Celebrations in My World

GROUNDHOG DAY

Lynn Peppas

Crabtree Publishing Company

www.crabtreebooks.com

Crabtree Publishing Company

www.crabtreebooks.com

Author: Lynn Peppas
Series and project editor: Sue Labella
Editor: Adrianna Morganelli
Proofreader: Reagan Miller
Photo research: Crystal Sikkens
Editorial director: Kathy Middleton
Design: Katherine Berti
  Ravinder Kumar (Q2AMEDIA)
Production coordinator and
  Prepress technician: Katherine Berti

Special thanks to:
Matteo and Giuliana Gervasio

Photographs:
Photos 12/Alamy: pages 28, 29
Associated Press: pages 12, 21, 22, 26
BigStockPhoto: page 4
Dreamstime: pages 8, 25
iStockPhoto: page 14
Margaret Amy Salter: cover, pages 1 (except
  groundhog), 27
Shutterstock: pages 1 (groundhog), 5, 6, 7, 9,
  10, 11, 13, 15, 16, 17, 18, 19, 20, 24, 30, 31
Wikipedia: Shari Chambers: page 23

Library and Archives Canada Cataloguing in Publication

Peppas, Lynn
    Groundhog Day / Lynn Peppas.

(Celebrations in my world)
Includes index.
Issued also in an electronic format.
ISBN 978-0-7787-4926-4 (bound).--ISBN 978-0-7787-4933-2 (pbk.)

    1. Groundhog Day--Juvenile literature. 2. Woodchuck--Juvenile
literature. I. Title. II. Series: Celebrations in my world

GT4995.G76P46 2010   j394.261   C2010-902749-3

Library of Congress Cataloging-in-Publication Data

Peppas, Lynn.
    Groundhog Day / Lynn Peppas.
       p. cm. -- (Celebrations in my world)
    Includes index.
    ISBN 978-0-7787-4933-2 (pbk. : alk. paper) -- ISBN 978-0-7787-4926-4
(reinforced library binding : alk. paper) -- ISBN 978-1-4271-9443-5
(electronic (pdf))
    1. Groundhog Day--Juvenile literature. 2. Woodchuck--Juvenile
literature. I. Title. II. Series.

GT4995.G76.P47 2010
394.261--dc22
                                        2010016405

Crabtree Publishing Company

www.crabtreebooks.com   1-800-387-7650

Printed in Hong Kong/042011/BK20110304

Published in Canada
Crabtree Publishing
616 Welland Ave.
St. Catharines, Ontario
L2M 5V6

Published in the United States
Crabtree Publishing
PMB 59051
350 Fifth Avenue, 59th Floor
New York, New York 10118

Published in the United Kingdom
Crabtree Publishing
Maritime House
Basin Road North, Hove
BN41 1WR

Published in Australia
Crabtree Publishing
386 Mt. Alexander Rd.
Ascot Vale (Melbourne)
VIC 3032

Contents

What Is Groundhog Day? 4
What Is a Groundhog? 6
Underground Homes 8
Hibernation 10
Winter Celebration 12
A Groundhog's Prediction 14
History of Groundhog Day 16
A Famous Groundhog 18
Punxsutawney, Pennsylvania 20
Canada's Famous Groundhog 22
Wiarton, Ontario 24
Other Groundhog Days 26
Groundhog Day: The Movie 28
Groundhog Day Quiz 30
Glossary and Index 32

What Is Groundhog Day?

Groundhog Day is a fun holiday. It is held every year on February 2. Some groups of people raise groundhogs just for this holiday.

- Groundhog Day always falls on February 2.

DID YOU KNOW?

Only a few countries celebrate Groundhog Day, including the United States and Canada.

These animals make Groundhog Day a special event. On this day, people watch to see whether or not a groundhog sees its **shadow**.

It helps them guess when spring will come. Others listen to or watch reports on what the groundhog saw.

Special groundhogs are kept and used every year on this holiday.

What Is a Groundhog?

Groundhogs are cute, grayish-brown, furry animals. The groundhog is one of the largest animals in the **rodent** family. Mice, squirrels, and guinea pigs also belong to the rodent family.

- What other animals does a groundhog remind you of?

6

Groundhogs look cute, but they are wild animals.

Groundhogs eat plants, insects, and seeds. They can weigh up to nine pounds (four kg).

Most groundhogs live in the wild. All groundhogs live in Canada and the United States. They are not found in any other country. Their sharp teeth can bite through wood. Wild groundhogs are not cuddly like a pet.

DID YOU KNOW?

Groundhogs are also called woodchucks, whistle pigs, land beavers, and marmots.

7

Underground Homes

Groundhogs build homes called **burrows**. They make their homes in flat, wide-open country areas. A burrow is an underground tunnel and living space.

A groundhog builds its home underground.

Can you say this famous **tongue twister**? "How much wood would a woodchuck chuck, if a woodchuck could chuck wood?"

Groundhogs use thick claws to dig their burrows.

A groundhog's burrow can have up to five different entrance holes. Groundhogs use their burrows to store food, raise families, and for protection from other animals.

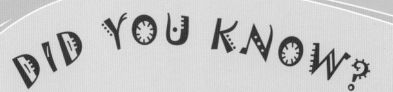

DID YOU KNOW?

The answer to the tongue twister is that a woodchuck can chuck about 700 lbs (317 kg) of dirt when it digs out a burrow!

Hibernation

Groundhogs **hibernate** in the winter. Hibernate means to sleep deeply for a long time—much longer than when you sleep at night.

- Groundhogs sleep for many months during the winter.

10

Other animals such as bears and squirrels hibernate, too. Groundhogs hibernate in burrows to help keep them safe from other animals.

Animals hibernate during cold winter months. It helps them live through winter when there is very little to eat.

Bats hibernate in caves or other safe places during the winter.

DID YOU KNOW?

Groundhogs usually hibernate from October to March or April. They wake up many times, such as on February 2, and then go back to sleep.

11

Winter Celebration

Groundhog Day is a winter celebration. Winter is the coldest season. Winter days have the shortest amount of daylight and the longest amount of darkness at night.

People enjoy dressing warmly and gathering for winter festivals, such as on Groundhog Day.

DID YOU KNOW?

Groundhogs grow to be 26 inches (66 cm) long and weigh up to nine pounds (4 kg)—the size of a cat or small dog.

There are fun things to do in winter, but many people cannot wait for spring and the warmer weather it brings.

In North America, winter starts on December 20 or 21 and ends on March 20 or 21.

By February, people are tired of the cold weather. They can hardly wait until spring and the warmer weather arrives.

A Groundhog's Prediction

On Groundhog Day, the groundhog helps make a **prediction**. A prediction is a guess about something that will happen in the future.

- On a sunny day, you can see your own shadow.

DID YOU KNOW?

Groundhogs do not really know when spring will come. Groundhog Day is just a fun time to guess about when spring will arrive.

On February 2, people watch a groundhog come out of its burrow. If it is a sunny day, the groundhog will see its shadow. The shadow scares the groundhog, and it runs back to its burrow and sleeps for six more weeks. Some people believe this means we will have six more weeks of winter.

If it is cloudy on Groundhog Day, the groundhog will not see its shadow. The groundhog will come out of its burrow. Some people believe this means spring is coming soon.

Can you see where the groundhog's shadow is?

History of Groundhog Day

Long ago on February 2, people from **Europe** celebrated a **religious** holiday called Candlemas. If it was sunny on Candlemas, people believed that more winter weather was on the way. If it was a cloudy day, people believed it was a sign that spring was coming.

Crocuses are another sign that spring is here.

DID YOU KNOW?

Long ago, many people from Europe moved to America. They brought with them old **customs** that took place on Candlemas. The holiday is a lot like our Groundhog Day today!

Another Candlemas custom was to watch hibernating animals such as bears or badgers. If people saw these animals awaken, it meant that spring would soon be coming!

This badger lives in an underground burrow.

A Famous Groundhog

America's most famous groundhog is named Punxsutawney Phil. His nickname is Punxsy Phil. He lives in Punxsutawney, Pennsylvania.

Punxsutawney Phil has his own burrow.

DID YOU KNOW?

Punxsutawney Phil was on the Oprah Winfrey Show in 1995.

Since 1887, Phil's predictions have been right 39% of the time.

He made the first prediction about spring over 100 years ago. **Legend** says that Punxsy Phil is more than 120 years old.

It says he is given a special potion each summer that makes him live for seven more years. But groundhogs do not live that long. Most live for two to seven years.

19

Punxsutawney, Pennsylvania

Punxsutawney, Pennsylvania, is home to the oldest Groundhog Day festival in the United States.

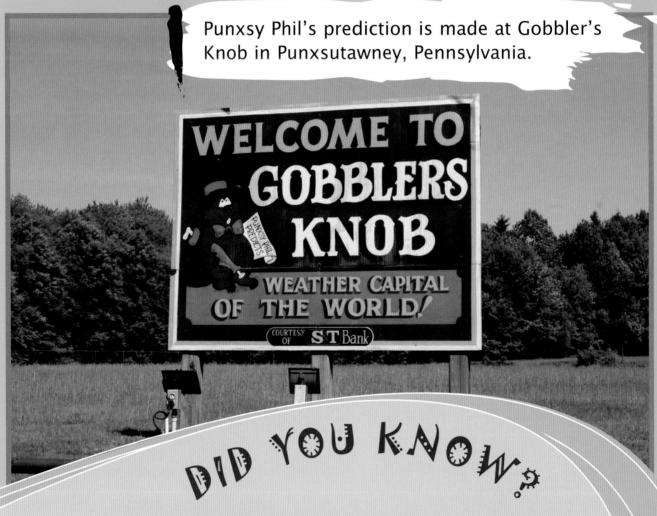

Punxsy Phil's prediction is made at Gobbler's Knob in Punxsutawney, Pennsylvania.

DID YOU KNOW?

Over 30,000 people visit Punxsutawney for the annual Groundhog Day festival. Besides Phil's prediction, there is special food and music for the event.

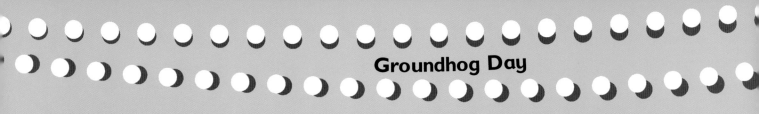

The festival has been celebrated there for over 100 years. A group of people called the Inner Circle carry out Groundhog Day customs there every year.

On February 2, the members of the Inner Circle dress up in tuxedos and top hats. They take Punxsy Phil to his burrow at Gobbler's Knob. Phil lives in a **terrarium** at the local library.

Inner Circle members take care of Punxsy Phil all year long.

Canada's Famous Groundhog

Wiarton Willie was Canada's most famous groundhog. He began making predictions in the 1980s.

- Wiarton Willie was an all-white, **albino** groundhog.

DID YOU KNOW?

Wiarton Willie was the oldest known groundhog. He lived to be 22 years old.

Most groundhogs have brown fur and black eyes. Willie was an albino groundhog. Albino means his fur was white and his eyes were pink. Today, another albino groundhog named Wee Willie makes the yearly prediction in Wiarton.

In 1995, a statue of Wiarton Willie was made. It is carved from more than four tons (3.6 metric tons) of white stone. It stands in Bluewater Park—the same park where Willie made his prediction on February 2.

This statue is called "Willie Emerging," and can be found in Willie's hometown of Wiarton, Ontario.

23

Wiarton, Ontario

Groundhog Day has been celebrated in Wiarton, Ontario, for over 50 years. It began when a man named Mac Mackenzie invited friends to a Groundhog Day celebration on February 2, 1956.

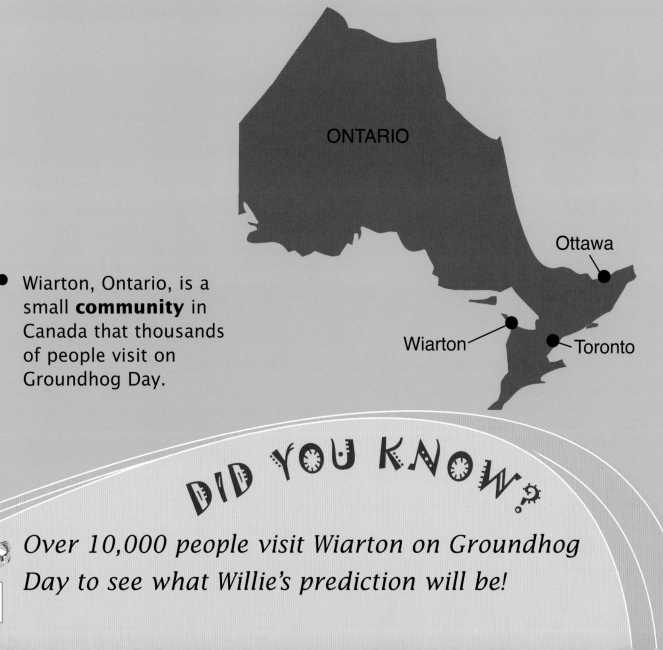

ONTARIO

Ottawa

- Wiarton, Ontario, is a small **community** in Canada that thousands of people visit on Groundhog Day.

Wiarton

Toronto

DID YOU KNOW?

Over 10,000 people visit Wiarton on Groundhog Day to see what Willie's prediction will be!

Today, the Groundhog Day festival in Wiarton is one week long. There are dances, sports, live music, and food events. The most important event is Willie's prediction!

People enjoy sleigh rides and other activities during the Groundhog Day celebrations in Wiarton.

Other Groundhog Days

Other cities in North America hold Groundhog Day celebrations, too. In the United States, a groundhog named Staten Island Chuck makes his prediction in New York City.

Woody the woodchuck predicts when spring will come in Michigan.

DID YOU KNOW?

Some communities hold Groundhog Day parades such as in Essex, Connecticut.

These children are making Groundhog Day crafts.

In Georgia, a groundhog named General Beauregard Lee makes the prediction for an early or late spring. Canada has other famous groundhogs too, such as Shubenacadie Sam in Nova Scotia.

Not all cities have Groundhog Day celebrations. Many wait to learn about the groundhog's prediction from TV, the radio, or in newspapers. Some schools celebrate by making Groundhog Day crafts.

27

Groundhog Day: The Movie

There has even been a movie called *Groundhog Day*. It is a comedy that first came out in 1993. A comedy means it is a funny movie.

Actor Bill Murray announces Punxsy Phil's prediction in the movie *Groundhog Day*.

DID YOU KNOW?

Some communities show the movie, Groundhog Day, *at their local theaters to celebrate the holiday.*

In the movie, actor Bill Murray plays a grouchy weatherman named "Phil." Phil travels to Punxsutawney, Pennsylvania, to report on the Groundhog Day event.

He cannot leave because of a snowstorm. The next morning, he starts living the same Groundhog Day over and over again.

● Actor Bill Murray in a scene from the movie, *Groundhog Day*

29

Groundhog Day Quiz

1. What is the name of America's most famous groundhog?

2. What is the name of Canada's most famous groundhog?

Groundhogs have strong front teeth that let them cut through wood.

DID YOU KNOW?

The toy company Ty Inc. released a special Punxsutawney Phil Beanie Baby™ to celebrate Groundhog Day.

A groundhog is the only animal that has a holiday named after it.

3. What is another name for a groundhog?

4. What two countries do groundhogs live in?

5. When do we celebrate Groundhog Day?

5. February 2

4. United States and Canada

3. whistle pig, woodchuck, land beaver, or marmot

2. Wiarton Willie

1. Punxsutawney Phil

Answers:

31

Glossary

albino A person or animal with pale or colorless skin, eyes, and hair

burrow A hole dug in the ground by animals for shelter

community A group of people living together in one area

custom The way things are done by a group of people for many years

Europe A continent that stretches from the Atlantic Ocean to Asia and includes countries such as France, Italy, United Kingdom, and many others

hibernate To sleep deeply during winter months

legend A story that has been handed down from the past

prediction A guess about something that will happen in the future

religious Relating to a person's belief in God

rodent An animal such as a mouse or beaver that gnaws with large front teeth

shadow An image made by an object blocking the sun's rays

terrarium A large glass shelter filled with dirt

tongue twister A group of sentences that are hard to say correctly

Index

badger 17

burrow 8, 9, 11, 15

Candlemas 16, 17

hibernate 10, 11, 15, 16, 17

prediction 14, 19, 20, 22, 23, 25, 26, 27

Punxsutawney Phil 18, 19, 20, 21, 28

shadow 5, 14, 15

spring 13, 14, 15, 17, 26, 27

Wiarton Willie 22, 23, 24, 25

winter 10, 11, 12, 13, 15, 16

woodchuck 7, 8 ,9